Friday 4 PM

*The Metrics & Viability
Of Sales Calling
Late on a Friday Afternoon*

by Robert James

Copyright © 2013 Robert James
All rights reserved.
ISBN-13: 978-1494458522
ISBN-10: 1494458527

To Mary, Robert and Lindsay.   Always.

CONTENTS

INTRODUCTION 7

TARGETS 9

METHOD 11

CONTACT RATE 13

RESULTS 15

COMPARISON 17

DIFFICULT-TO-REACH PROSPECTS 21

PUTTING IT TO THE TEST 23

THE CONCLUSION 25

APPENDIX: TOTAL ATTEMPTS AND TARGETS 27

ABOUT THE AUTHOR 29

ALSO BY ROBERT JAMES 31

Robert James

INTRODUCTION

It's 4PM on a Friday.

Is it worth your time to do some sales calling and emailing to prospective clients? If you spend the next hour making calls and sending out emails, will you reach your targets?

Is there any possibility of reaching anyone? Or talking to those hard to reach managers who didn't respond earlier in the week? Of finding any kind of lead?

Or will you be wasting your time?

I spent two years analyzing these very questions.

What follows are analyses, summaries and data on sales calling and emailing (i.e. prospecting) on a Friday at 4 PM. The information is presented in succinct summaries with some supporting evidence, so you can quickly make a determination. It is based on more than 200 calls and emails over a 2 year period and is an expansion on the case study presented on my [Sales Notes Blog]().

I welcome your questions, comments or feedback to [fromthedeskofrobertjames@yahoo.com]().

Robert James

TARGETS

Who did I target? More than 150 Managers and Directors over a two year period.

Approximately 60% of the targets were new prospects (i.e. someone I'd not talked to before) and 40% involved follow up calls to a previous conversation.

Calls and emails to existing clients or managers where I had a good *existing* relationship were not included.

Robert James

METHOD

Over 200 calls (202) and emails were tracked.

My general method was to start with a call, followed by an email if a prospect did not answer the phone or said they were in a meeting.

Because I'd discovered previously that a voice mail does not increase the success of an email (see SELLING: USING VOICE MAIL), very few voice mails were left.

Every call, email and result was logged in a spreadsheet. A manager who stated they were too busy to talk was recorded as *not* reached.

CONTACT RATE

The first step is – always – reaching people. You can't sell if you don't reach prospective clients to sell to.

So what was my success rate for attempting to reach prospects at 4 PM on a Friday?

I reached 16% (about one in six) of my targeted prospects by phone or email at this time.

RESULTS

Reaching someone is one thing, but the results are what really matter. If you talk to 100 people but no one is interested, that doesn't really help.

What were the results when I reached someone late on a Friday?

13% (about one in eight) of the prospects I reached provided me with a genuine lead, 13% said they were not interested, and the remaining 74% gave me a variation of somewhere "maybe," such as "Send me information," "Not looking at this time" or "contact me again in a few months."

COMPARISON

Clearly, prospects can be reached late on a Friday afternoon. And a few will even give me an opportunity to work with them.

But how does this compare to other days and times?

That is, was late Friday as good (or better) of a time to prospect as other days and times of the week?

Or were the results actually worse, meaning I was better off leaving a little early on Friday and prospecting a different day or time of the week?

I compared the data from my Friday 4 PM hunting efforts to the 7,000+ business development activities I tracked for the remainder of the week during the same two year period. And the contact rates for Friday are almost identical to the overall statistics, although Friday afternoon produced slightly better *results*.

If I made a call or sent an email any other time of the week, I reached 16% of my targeted prospects. This was exactly the same percentage as a Friday afternoon at 4 PM. Of the managers I reached during the week, about 11% of the time they gave me a lead, which was a slight *decrease* from Friday afternoon.

Is this a measurable difference? Or so slight as not to matter.

You be the judge...

Using the numbers above, if over a period of time you called 200 people on a Friday afternoon, you'd reach 32 and 4 would give you a lead. If you made those

200 calls at other times during the week, you'd reach 32 and 3 or 4 (actually 3.5) would give you a lead.

So there is a difference, but it's slight.

Robert James

DIFFICULT-TO-REACH PROSPECTS

A potential value in calling late on a Friday is reaching prospects who are hard to reach other times of the week. That is, if you call late on a Friday is there a better chance of reaching those hard-to-reach prospects who rarely answer the phone the rest of the week?

In short, yes.

In general, I had a 16% chance of reaching a prospect on Friday at 4 PM. Of those I attempted to reach, there was a 12% chance of reaching them any other time of the week. And of those I reached, there was a 15% chance of reaching them the rest of the week.

So you *are* more likely to reach a hard-to-reach prospect late on a Friday.

PUTTING IT TO THE TEST

Do these results hold water in a limited follow up test?

On a recent Friday afternoon at 4 PM, I targeted 10 managers. Four of these managers I had reached before and six were cold calls. For each manager, I placed a call and then if they didn't answer I sent them an immediate email.

The results?

I reached two by phone (not including one who said he was in a meeting). A third responded over the weekend to email. Two of these were new prospects and one was a manager I'd reached before.

Of the three I reached, one said he might have a need in three months (during the next budget cycle), explained why he'd have a need and suggested we set up a time to meet in a couple of months. The other two said they didn't have a need at that time but they might in the future so to continue checking in every few months.

This converted to a 17% success rate (10 calls plus 8 emails to reach 3 managers) with one possible lead.

This is what I would expect based on the historical averages for Friday at 4 PM...

THE CONCLUSION

One of the biggest fears of experienced Business Developers is wasting time – they hate wasting time on something that has little chance of producing results.

But have no fear – late on a Friday is a good time to call.

You'll reach as many managers as you would any other time and you are even slightly *more* likely to find a lead. As an added bonus, you have a better chance of managers who are hard to reach other times of the week.

So postpone that golf game for an extra hour and log a few more calls before closing your laptop for the weekend.

Over time, you'll be glad you did.

Robert James

APPENDIX: TOTAL ATTEMPTS AND TARGETS

Total Attempts Over 2 Years = 7,284
Total Prospects Over 2 Years = 937
Total Friday 4 PM Attempts Over 2 Years = 202
Total Prospects Friday 4 PM Over 2 Years = 166

Robert James

ABOUT THE AUTHOR

Robert James has nearly 15 years of Experience as a Business Developer, Account Manager, Sales Executive and Sales Manager. He *loves* the science of Business Development. His research is based on 10 years of sales analysis (data) and he writes for the fun of it. His blog is found at Sales Notes and a list of his other books are on the following page(s).

Suggestions, comments and additional insight? Is there research you'd like to see? You may reach him at fromthedeskofrobertjames@yahoo.com.

Please note he has a day job (most recently as a player-coach with both an individual and team quota) so there may be a delay in responses.

Robert James

ALSO BY ROBERT JAMES

Sales

Sales Notes (Blog)

Selling: Using Voice Mail

The Reluctant Business Developer

The Technical Staffing Account Manager's Playbook

For Fun

The 10-Minute Pompeii

My Friend Bergler

www.ingramcontent.com/pod-product-compliance
Lightning Source LLC
Chambersburg PA
CBHW070732180526
45167CB00004B/1715